A Year to Re:

1954

For Those Whose Hearts Belong to 1954

Celebrating your year

1954

A memorable year for

Contents
Introduction: A Glimpse into 1954

Introduction: A Glimpse into 1954..5

Chapter 1: Politics and Leading Events around the World

1.1 The Global Stage in 1954: Where Were You?....................6

1.2 Leaders and Statesmen: Movers and Shakers of '54......13

Activity: Historical Crossword Test Your Knowledge of'54...17

Chapter 2: The Iconic Movies, TV Shows, and Awards

2.1 Memorable Films of '54...19

2.2 TV Shows That Captivated the Nation.............................26

2.3 Prestigious Film Awards and Honors.............................30

Activity: Movie and TV Show Trivia Quiz - How Well Do You Know '54 Entertainment?..32

Chapter 3: Music: Top Songs, Albums, and Awards

3.1 Chart-Toppers and Musical Trends.............................35

3.2 Notable Albums and Song Releases.............................39

Activity: Music Lyrics Challenge - Guess the Song Lyrics from '54...40

Chapter 4: Sports in 1954

4.1 Sporting Achievements and Memorable Victories...........41

4.2 American Sports: Champions and Championship Moments...47

Activity: Sports Trivia - Test Your Knowledge of 1954 Sports History...50

Chapter 5: Fashion, and Popular Leisure Activities

5.1 What the World Wore in '54...52

5.2 Entertainment and Hobbies 60

Activity: Fashion Design Coloring Page - Create Your '54-Inspired Outfit...64

Chapter 6: Technological Advancements and Popular Cars
6.1 Innovations That Shaped the Future.................................65
6.2 The Automobiles of '54...68
Activity: Cars 1954 - Wordsearch....................................73

Chapter 7: Stats and the Cost of Things
7.1 Cost of Living in 1954...75
7.2 Inflation and Its Effects...78
Activity: 1954 Guess the price......................................79

Chapter 8: Iconic Advertisements of 1954
8.1 Remembering Vintage Ads..80
8.2 Slogans That Stood the Test of Time............................85
Activity: Design your own slogan...................................87

Special gift for readers..88
Activity answers...92

Introduction

A Year to Remember - 1954
For Those Whose Hearts Belong to 1954

To our cherished readers who hold a special connection to the year 1954, whether it's because you were born in this remarkable year, celebrated a milestone, or hold dear memories from that time, this book is a tribute to you and your unique connection to an unforgettable era.

In the pages that follow, we invite you to embark on a captivating journey back to 1954, a year of profound historical significance. For those with a personal connection to this year, it holds a treasure trove of memories, stories, and experiences that shaped the world and touched your lives.

Throughout this book, we've woven together the tapestry of 1954, providing historical insights, personal stories, and interactive activities that allow you to relive and celebrate the significance of this special year.

As you turn the pages and immerse yourself in the events and culture of 1954, we hope you'll find moments of nostalgia, inspiration, and the opportunity to rekindle cherished memories of this extraordinary year.

This book is dedicated to you, our readers, who share a unique bond with 1954. May it bring you joy, enlightenment, and a deeper connection to the rich tapestry of history that weaves through your lives.

With warm regards,

Edward Art Lab.

Chapter 1:
Politics and Leading Events around the World

In the midst of the mid-20th century, the year 1954 bore witness to a world in constant flux. Political landscapes were shifting, global tensions were simmering, and leaders were navigating uncharted territory. Chapter 1 unravels the political tapestry of this pivotal year, exploring the major events and influential figures who shaped the world stage.

1.1 The Global Stage in 1954: Where Were You?

Senator Joseph McCarthy Censured, Ending Witch Hunt

In a pivotal moment in 1954, Senator Joseph McCarthy faced a reckoning as his aggressive pursuit of alleged communists came to an end. The U.S. Senate, alarmed by McCarthy's tactics and disregard for due process, censured him. This formal reprimand marked the conclusion of his infamous witch hunt for communists within the government and other sectors of American society. McCarthy's fall from grace was a significant moment in U.S. political history and a reminder of the importance of upholding democratic principles and civil liberties.

Vietnam: The First Indo-China War Ends in 1954

In 1954, the First Indochina War, a prolonged struggle over Vietnam's control, concluded. The conflict pitted French colonial forces against the communist-led Viet Minh, with a turning point being the Battle of Dien Bien Phu. Viet Minh's victory led to the surrender of French forces in May 1954. The war's end was formalized by the Geneva Accords, which temporarily divided Vietnam along the 17th parallel, foreshadowing the later Vietnam War.

The Supreme Court's Landmark Ruling: Brown v. Board of Education

In 1954, the U.S. Supreme Court issued a groundbreaking decision in the case of Brown v. Board of Education. This ruling declared racial segregation in public schools unconstitutional, overturning the "separate but equal" doctrine. The decision had a profound impact, sparking the dismantling of segregation in various public facilities and marking a significant victory for the civil rights movement. It remains a pivotal moment in U.S. history, symbolizing the ongoing fight for racial equality.

Ellis Island: The End of an Era

In 1954, Ellis Island, a symbol of hope and opportunity for millions of immigrants, closed its doors as a point of immigration. Located in New York Harbor, Ellis Island had been the gateway to America for over six decades, processing and welcoming immigrants from around the world. However, changing immigration laws and declining numbers of arrivals led to its closure. While it ceased its role as an immigration processing center, Ellis Island remains a historic site and a testament to the immigrant experience in the United States. It stands as a reminder of the nation's rich and diverse heritage, shaped by the dreams and aspirations of those who passed through its gates.

President Eisenhower Signs Social Security Bill

In 1954, President Dwight D. Eisenhower signed a landmark piece of legislation into law, shaping the future of
social welfare in the United States. The new social security bill, funded by both employers and employees, aimed
to strengthen the nation's social safety net. This comprehensive legislation expanded social security coverage and
increased benefits for retirees and disabled individuals.
It also marked a significant step toward addressing the
needs of an aging population. President Eisenhower's sig-
nature on this bill reflected a commitment to ensuring the
economic well-being and security of American citizens,
setting the stage for the evolving landscape of social programs in the years to come.

"Under God" Added to the U.S. Pledge of Allegiance

Pledge of Allegiance

"I pledge allegiance to the Flag of the United States of America and to the Republic for which it stands, One Nation under God, indivisible, with Liberty and Justice for all."

In 1954, the United States made a significant addition to its Pledge of Allegiance, forever altering the oath of loyalty that generations of Americans had recited. The phrase "under God" was introduced to the pledge, making it a reflection of the nation's religious beliefs. This change was initiated during the Cold War era when the United States sought to distinguish itself from the officially atheistic Soviet Union. The altered pledge was seen as a way to emphasize America's religious and moral values.

The new wording, "I pledge allegiance to the flag of the United States of America, and to the republic for which it stands, one nation under God, indivisible, with liberty and justice for all," was not without controversy, sparking debates about the separation of church and state. Nevertheless, "under God" has remained a part of the U.S. Pledge of Allegiance, a reminder of the nation's historical and cultural connection to religious principles.

Bikini Atoll - Operation Castle

1. Operation Castle begins in March.
2. It was a series of nuclear bomb tests conducted by the United States' Atomic Energy Commission and the Department of Defense which took place on Bikini Atoll.
3. The first explosion, Castle Bravo, was the first test of "dry fuel" thermonuclear bombs which used lithium deuteride that did not require cumbersome cryogenic equipment to keep the fuel liquefied as in previous versions.
4. The 15-megaton explosion of Castle Bravo was about three times more powerful than expected, causing mass amounts of contamination and radiation exposure to nearby island inhabitants, naval ships, fishermen, and test personnel.
5. It prompted international cries for a ban on atmospheric thermonuclear testing.

1.2 Leaders and Statesmen: Movers and Shakers of '54

The year 1954 saw a constellation of remarkable leaders and statesmen making their mark on the global stage. These individuals played pivotal roles in shaping the course of events in their respective nations and beyond.

Dwight D. Eisenhower:

Serving as the 34th President of the United States, Eisenhower was a steady hand during the tumultuous era of the Cold War. His leadership focused on containing communism while promoting economic prosperity and civil rights at home.

Nikita Khrushchev:

As the First Secretary of the Communist Party of the Soviet Union, Khrushchev was a key figure during the Cold War. His leadership style was marked by a confrontational stance against the West, including the famous "Kitchen Debate" with U.S. Vice President Richard Nixon.

Ho Chi Minh:

Ho Chi Minh led the Viet Minh forces in their quest for Vietnamese independence. His leadership culminated in the victory at Dien Bien Phu and the end of French colonial rule in Vietnam.

Gamal Abdel Nasser:

Nasser emerged as a prominent leader in Egypt. As the second President of Egypt, he championed pan-Arabism and played a pivotal role in the Suez Crisis, asserting Egyptian sovereignty over the Suez Canal.

Jawaharlal Nehru:

Nehru, the first Prime Minister of India, was a visionary leader. He focused on nation-building, non-alignment in the Cold War, and fostering democracy in the world's largest democracy.

Winston Churchill:

Though no longer Prime Minister, Churchill remained a statesman and influential voice in British politics. His speeches continued to inspire as he warned against the dangers of the Cold War and the nuclear arms race.

Juan Perón:

Perón, the President of Argentina, was a charismatic leader with a significant following. His populist policies shaped Argentina's political landscape during the mid-20th century.

Activity: Historical Crossword

Test Your Knowledge of '54

Are you ready to challenge your knowledge of the significant events and key figures of 1954? Here's a crossword puzzle that will test your understanding of the historic year.

ACROSS

1. Ellis Island, a symbol of hope for immigrants, closed its doors as a point of immigration in 1954, located in New York

_____.

2. Senator Joseph McCarthy's tactics faced a formal _____ in 1954, ending his witch hunt for communists.

3. This leader of the Viet Minh played a crucial role in achieving Vietnamese independence in 1954.

4. The first Prime Minister of India, known for his non-alignment policy during the Cold War.

5. In 1954, the United States added the phrase "under God" to the Pledge of _____.

DOWN

1. In 1954, the U.S. Supreme Court issued a landmark decision declaring racial segregation in public schools unconstitutional, known as _____ v. Board of Education

2. The First Secretary of the Communist Party of the Soviet Union during the Cold War.

4. President Dwight D. Eisenhower signed a comprehensive social security bill into law in 1954, aiming to strengthen the nation's social _____ net.

6. The Battle of Dien Bien Phu marked a turning point in the First Indochina War, leading to the surrender of French _____.

8. Egyptian President who championed pan-Arabism and played a pivotal role in the Suez Crisis in 1954.

Enjoy the crossword!

Chapter 2:
The Iconic Movies, TV Shows, and Awards

2.1 Memorable Films of '54

The year 1954 witnessed a plethora of iconic and memorable films that left an indelible mark on the world of cinema. Hollywood delivered a range of cinematic experiences, from timeless classics to groundbreaking innovations.

White Christmas:

Directed by Michael Curtiz and starring Bing Crosby and Danny Kaye, "White Christmas" is a heartwarming holiday musical that features the classic song of the same name. It tells the story of two World War II veterans who team up with a sister act to save a failing Vermont inn.

Rear Window:

Directed by Alfred Hitchcock and starring James Stewart and Grace Kelly, "Rear Window" is a suspenseful thriller that follows a wheelchair-bound photographer who becomes convinced he's witnessed a murder in a neighboring apartment. The film is celebrated for its innovative use of a single set.

On the Waterfront:

On The Waterfront

Music Composed by **LEONARD BERNSTEIN**

Directed by Elia Kazan and starring Marlon Brando, Karl Malden, and Eva Marie Saint, this powerful drama explores corruption on the docks and the moral dilemma faced by a longshoreman who wants to expose it. Marlon Brando's performance is particularly iconic.

River of No Return:

Directed by Otto Preminger and starring Robert Mitchum and Marilyn Monroe, this Western adventure film follows a man, his son, and a saloon singer as they navigate dangerous river rapids in the wilds of Canada.

The Caine Mutiny:

Directed by Edward Dmytryk and starring Humphrey Bogart, José Ferrer, and Van Johnson, this courtroom drama revolves around the mutiny aboard a U.S. Navy minesweeper during World War II. Humphrey Bogart's portrayal of the mentally unstable Captain Queeg is a standout performance.

20,000 Leagues Under the Sea:

Directed by Richard Fleischer and based on Jules Verne's novel, this adventure film follows a group of men who embark on a journey to track down a mysterious sea monster, only to discover the advanced submarine Nautilus and its enigmatic captain, Nemo.

A Star Is Born:

Directed by George Cukor and starring Judy Garland and James Mason, this musical drama tells the story of a young singer's rise to fame and the toll it takes on her relationship with an aging actor. Judy Garland's performance is considered one of her best.

2.2 TV Shows That Captivated the Nation

The dawn of the television era brought forth a wave of captivating shows that became an integral part of American households. In 1954, television sets flickered to life with a diverse range of programming that catered to the tastes and interests of viewers across the nation. Let's journey back to the small screen wonders of '54:

1. "Walt Disney's Wonderful World of Color"

This anthology television series, hosted by Walt Disney himself, premiered in 1954. It was initially titled "Disneyland" but later became known as the "Walt Disney's Wonderful World of Color" due to its innovative use of color television. The show featured a mix of animated and live-action segments, along with behind-the-scenes looks at Disney's creative process. It was a groundbreaking program that brought Disney's magic into people's homes.

2. "Father Knows Best"

Starring Robert Young and Jane Wyatt, "Father Knows Best" was a beloved family sitcom that depicted the lives of the Andersons, a typical American family living in the Midwest. The series revolved around the challenges and humorous situations that arose within the family, with the patriarch, Jim Anderson, often providing guidance and life lessons. It resonated with audiences and became an enduring classic of the era.

3. "The Mickey Rooney Show"

Also known as "Hey, Mulligan," this sitcom starred Mickey Rooney as Mickey Mulligan, a lovable and mischievous mailroom clerk working at a large New York City hotel. The show followed Mickey's adventures as he navigated his job and interacted with various eccentric characters. Mickey Rooney's comedic talents and charm made the show a hit with viewers.

4. "Annie Oakley"

"Annie Oakley" was a Western television series starring Gail Davis as the legendary sharpshooter Annie Oakley. The show depicted Annie's adventures as a skilled markswoman who helped maintain law and order in the Old West. It was notable for featuring a strong and capable female lead character in a traditionally male-dominated genre.

2.3 Prestigious Film Awards and Honors

Best Picture: "From Here to Eternity"

Best Director: Fred Zinnemann for "From Here to Eternity"

Best Actor: William Holden for "Stalag 17"

Best Actress: Audrey Hepburn for "Roman Holiday"

Best Original Screenplay: Charles Brackett, Walter Reisch, and Richard L. Breen for "Titanic"

Best Film Editing: Elmo Williams and Harry W. Gerstad for "High Noon"

Best Sound Recording: Leslie I. Carey for "The War of the Worlds"

Best Documentary (Short Subject): "The Living Desert"

Honorary Award: George Alfred Mitchell, the producer of "The House in the Middle," for his imaginative use of standard materials and equipment in the production of the film.

Activity:
Movie and TV Show Trivia Quiz
How Well Do You Know '54 Entertainment?

Instructions: Test your knowledge of 1954 entertainment by answering the following questions based on the information provided in Chapter 2 of the book.

Movies (Questions 1-5):

1. Which iconic holiday film from 1954 features the classic song "White Christmas"?
a) Rear Window
b) River of No Return
c) White Christmas
d) A Star Is Born

2. Who directed the suspenseful thriller "Rear Window" in 1954?
a) Alfred Hitchcock
b) Michael Curtiz
c) Elia Kazan
d) Richard Fleischer

3. Which film explores corruption on the docks and stars Marlon Brando in a powerful role?
a) On the Waterfront
b) The Caine Mutiny
c) River of No Return
d) 20,000 Leagues Under the Sea

4. In "River of No Return," which famous actress starred alongside Robert Mitchum?

a) Grace Kelly

b) Audrey Hepburn

c) Marilyn Monroe

d) Judy Garland

5. Who played the mentally unstable Captain Queeg in the film "The Caine Mutiny"?

a) Humphrey Bogart

b) James Stewart

c) Marlon Brando

d) Robert Mitchum

TV Shows (Questions 6-9):

6. What was the title of the television series hosted by Walt Disney that made innovative use of color television?

a) Walt Disney's World of Imagination

b) Disney's Colorful Adventures

c) Walt Disney's Wonderful World of Color

d) The Magical World of Disney

7. "Father Knows Best" depicted the lives of which fictional American family?

a) The Smiths

b) The Johnsons

c) The Andersons

d) The Parkers

8. In "The Mickey Rooney Show," what was the occupation of Mickey Mulligan, the main character?

a) Mailroom clerk

b) Detective

c) Doctor

d) Teacher

9. Who portrayed the legendary sharpshooter Annie Oakley in the Western TV series "Annie Oakley"?
a) Gail Davis
b) Grace Kelly
c) Judy Garland
d) Audrey Hepburn

Awards (Questions 10-11):
10. Which film won the Academy Award for Best Picture in 1954?
a) Roman Holiday
b) Rear Window
c) White Christmas
d) From Here to Eternity

11. Who received an Honorary Award in 1954 for imaginative use of standard materials and equipment in the production of the film "The House in the Middle"?
a) Alfred Hitchcock
b) Walt Disney
c) George Alfred Mitchell
d) Audrey Hepburn

Scoring: Count how many correct answers you got out of 11 questions to see how well you know entertainment in 1954!

Chapter 3:
Music: Top Songs, Albums, and Awards

In the captivating realm of music, 1954 was a year that resonated with melodies and rhythms that not only filled the airwaves but also etched themselves into the hearts and memories of a generation. This chapter takes you on a harmonious
journey through the sounds and sensations of '54, exploring
the chart-toppers and the excellence celebrated in music
awards and honors.

3.1 Chart-Toppers and Musical Trends

In the vibrant world of music, 1954 was a year of transition
and transformation. The melodies that graced the airwaves
reflected the evolving tastes and emerging trends of the
time. This section opens a musical time capsule, allowing us
to relive the chart-toppers and explore the musical trends
that defined this dynamic year.

1. Chart-Topping Songs:

"Sh-Boom" - The Crew-Cuts:

The sound of doo-wop was on the rise, and "Sh-Boom" by The Crew-Cuts was at the forefront of this exciting musical movement. Its catchy rhythm and harmonious vocals had listeners snapping their fingers and swaying to the beat. This hit paved the way for the rock and roll explosion that would follow.

"Little Things Mean a Lot" - Kitty Kallen:

In a world hungry for heartfelt sentiment, Kitty Kallen's emotive voice struck a chord with audiences. "Little Things Mean a Lot" became an anthem of love and appreciation, reminding us that it's the small gestures that matter most.

"Mr. Sandman" - The Chordettes:

The Chordettes' enchanting harmonies transported listeners to a dreamy world where wishes came true. "Mr. Sandman" was not just a song; it was a lullaby that captured the hearts of many, making it a timeless classic.

2. The Dawn of Rock and Roll:

While doo-wop and ballads still held sway, 1954 was the year when rock and roll truly began to assert its dominance. Bill Haley & His Comets and a young Elvis Presley were starting to make waves with their electrifying sounds. The stage was set for a musical revolution.

3. The Jukebox Revolution:

Jukeboxes, those iconic fixtures of diners and soda shops, were filled with the latest hits of '54. Patrons eagerly selected their favorite tunes, turning jukeboxes into musical time machines. These coin-operated marvels played a significant role in sharing the sounds of the era.

4. Vinyl Dreams:

At home, vinyl records spun on turntables, bringing the magic of music into living rooms. The scratchy sound of a stylus tracing the grooves of a record became the soundtrack to countless evenings spent dancing, romancing, or simply savoring the joy of a song.

3.2 Notable Albums and Song Releases

Name	Author	Band / Singer
Clifford Brown and Max Roach	Clifford Brown and Max Roach	Clifford Brown and Max Roach
Chet Baker Sings	Chet Baker	Chet Baker
Louis Armstrong Plays W. C. Handy	Louis Armstrong	Louis Armstrong
Afro	Dizzy Gillespie	Dizzy Gillespie
Charlie Parker	Charlie Parker	Charlie Parker
Songs for Young Lovers	Frank Sinatra	Frank Sinatra
Mr. Sandman	The Chordettes	The Chordettes
Secret Love	Doris Day	Doris Day
Sh-Boom	The Crew-Cuts	The Crew-Cuts
Little Things Mean a Lot	Kitty Kallen	Kitty Kallen
Hey There	Rosemary Clooney	Rosemary Clooney

Activity:
Music Lyrics Challenge
Guess the Song Lyrics from '54

Instructions: Test your knowledge of classic song lyrics from the 1950s. Below are song titles from that era. Can you complete the lyrics of these songs? Fill in the blanks with the correct words to finish the lines.

1. "Mr. Sandman" by The Chordettes
"Mr. Sandman, bring me a dream, make him the _____ that I've ever seen."
2. "Secret Love" by Doris Day
"Now I shout it from the highest _____."
3. "Sh-Boom" by The Crew-Cuts
"Life could be a _____, if I could take you up in _____."
4. "Little Things Mean a Lot" by Kitty Kallen
"Send me the _____ that I cherish, like _____ in the rain."
5. "Hey There" by Rosemary Clooney
"Hey there, you with the _____ in your eyes, love never made a _____ of a fool."
Test your memory of these classic lyrics and see how well you remember these iconic songs from the 1950s!

Chapter 4: Sports in 1954:
A Journey Through the World of Athletics

4.1 Athletic Achievements and Memorable Victories

The year 1954 bore witness to exceptional athletic achievements that left an indelible mark on history. From the thrill of record-breaking feats to the enduring legacies of sports icons, this section explores the remarkable accomplishments of athletes who pushed the boundaries of human potential. Among these achievements are tales of endurance, strength, and skill that continue to inspire generations.

1. 1954 FIFA World Cup:

The 1954 World Cup, held in Switzerland, is known for West Germany's surprising triumph over Hungary in the final match, famously dubbed the "Miracle of Bern." This underdog victory had a profound impact, lifting the spirits of post-World War II West Germany and solidifying its place in football history. Legendary players like Ferenc Puskás and Helmut Rahn were key figures in this historic tournament, making it an iconic moment in football history.

2. Wimbledon Men's Tennis

Jul 2 Wimbledon Men's Tennis: Czech Jaroslav Drobný beats Ken Rosewall of Australia 13-11, 4-6, 6-2, 9-7 for his only Wimbledon singles title

Ken Rosewall

Jaroslav Drobný

3. Golf Tournament:

Mar 14 LPGA Titleholders Championship Women's Golf, Augusta CC: Louise Suggs wins her second Titleholders title by 7 strokes from Patty Berg

4. Tour de France:

Louison Bobet of France wins by 15' 49" from Ferdinand Kübler, for the second of his 3 consecutive wins

5. 58th Boston Marathon:

The winner of the 1954 Boston Marathon was Veikko Karvonen, a Finnish long-distance runner known for his endurance and competitive spirit. Karvonen crossed the finish line with an impressive time, showcasing his prowess as an athlete and solidifying his place in the annals of marathon history.

6. F1 World Champion

Aug 22 Juan Manuel Fangio of Argentina clinches his second Formula 1 World Drivers Championship by winning Swiss Grand Prix at Bremgarten in a Maserati

8. Boxing Title Fight

Heavyweight Boxing
Champion
Rocky Marciano

Boxer and World
Heavyweight Champion
Ezzard Charles

On June 17, Rocky Marciano secured a unanimous points decision victory over Ezzard Charles in his third world heavyweight boxing title defense at Yankee Stadium in New York City.

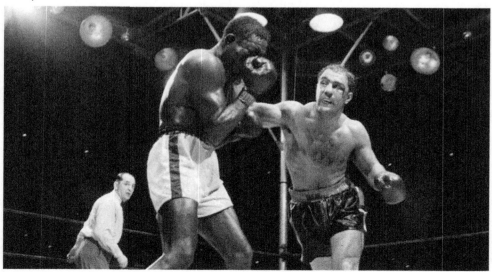

4.2 American Sports: Champions and Championship Moments

The American sports landscape in 1954 was characterized by triumphs, challenges, and unforgettable championship moments. From the baseball diamond to the football gridiron, American athletes displayed their prowess on the national stage. This section takes readers on a journey through the most iconic sporting events of the year, from historic World Series victories to thrilling NFL championships. It's a celebration of American sportsmanship and the enduring legacy of athletes who became household names.

1. World Series:

In the 1954 World Series, the New York Giants faced off against the Cleveland Indians. The Giants, led by stars like Willie Mays, swept the Indians in four games to win their fifth World Series title. One of the most memorable moments was Mays' incredible over-the-shoulder catch in Game 1. This Series is still celebrated for its drama and iconic plays.

2. NBA Finals:

In the 1954 NBA Finals, the Syracuse Nationals, led by star player Dolph Schayes, faced off against the Minneapolis Lakers, who had George Mikan as their key player. The Nationals defeated the Lakers in a thrilling seven-game series to secure their first NBA championship. This Finals match-up is remembered as a competitive and closely contested battle, marking a significant moment in NBA history.

3. National Football League:

In 1954, the NFL championship featured the Cleveland Browns facing off against the Detroit Lions. Led by star quarterback Otto Graham, the Browns secured their third consecutive championship with a decisive 56-10 victory over the Lions. The game showcased the Browns' dominance during this era and solidified Otto Graham's legacy as one of the NFL's greatest quarterbacks.

4. Stanley Cup Final, Olympia Stadium, Detroit, MI:

Detroit Red Wings beat Montreal Canadiens, 2-1 in OT for a 4-3 series victory

Activity: Sports Trivia
Test Your Knowledge of 1954 Sports History

Instructions: Put your sports knowledge to the test by answering the following questions about the memorable sports events and champions of 1954

1. Who won the 1954 FIFA World Cup, famously known as the "Miracle of Bern"?

a) Hungary

b) West Germany

c) Brazil

d) Italy

2. Which American baseball team won the 1954 World Series, led by star player Willie Mays?

a) New York Yankees

b) Brooklyn Dodgers

c) Cleveland Indians

d) New York Giants

3.In the 1954 NBAFinals,which team secured their first NBA championship by defeating the Minneapolis Lakers?

a) Boston Celtics

b) Syracuse Nationals

c) Los Angeles Lakers

d) Chicago Bulls

4. Who was the legendary Finnish long-distance runner that **won the 1954 Boston Marathon?**

a) Emil Zátopek

b) Paavo Nurmi

c) Veikko Karvonen

d) Hannes Kolehmainen

5. Which Argentine Formula 1 driver clinched his second Formula 1 World Drivers Championship in 1954?

a) Juan Manuel Fangio

b) Alberto Ascari

c) Stirling Moss

d) Mike Hawthorn

6. In the NFL championship of 1954, which team secured their third consecutive championship with a decisive victory over the Detroit Lions?

a) Green Bay Packers

b) Cleveland Browns

c) Chicago Bears

d) New York Giants

7. Who was the American heavyweight boxer who defeated Ezzard Charles in a unanimous points decision on June 17, 1954, at Yankee Stadium?

a) Muhammad Ali

b) Joe Louis

c) Rocky Marciano

d) Floyd Patterson

8. In the 1954 Stanley Cup Final, which team secured a 4-3 series victory with a dramatic overtime win?

a) Montreal Canadiens

b) Detroit Red Wings

c) Toronto Maple Leafs

d) Chicago Blackhawks

Chapter 5:
Fashion, and Popular Leisure Activities

5.1 What the World Wore in '54

The year 1954 marked an intriguing intersection of fashion, reflecting both the nostalgia of the post-World War II era and the early stirrings of the coming cultural revolution. Fashion in 1954 was characterized by a blend of timeless elegance and the beginning of new, daring trends. Let's take a look at what the world was wearing in '54:

Women's Fashion:

1. Iridescent Taffeta Dress:

Iridescent chromspun taffeta... crisp, richly colored acetate with changeable two-tone effect... keeps its color. Flattering neckline has pleated insert; rhinestone trim. Flared two-gore skirt back. Reinforced rayon velvet belt. Colors are sparkling deep blue or sparkling wine red.

2. Pencil Skirts:

Alongside the New Look, pencil skirts became a staple of women's wardrobes. These slim, straight skirts emphasized the hips and legs, offering a sleek and sophisticated look.

3. Gloves:

No outfit was complete without gloves in 1954. Women wore gloves for both day and evening occasions, often in coordinating colors with their outfits.

4. Hats:

Hats remained an essential accessory. Pillbox hats, popularized by Jacqueline Kennedy, were particularly in vogue. These small, flat-crowned hats were often worn tilted to one side.

Men's Fashion:

1. Wool Houndstooth Suit: So hard-finished and wrinkle-resistant it simply ignores wrinkles and wear. The dressy houndstooth pattern will win you many compliments with its high styled multicolor treatment. The tailoring and smooth fitting lines put you at your best. Two button, single breasted, three patch pocket styling. Doubles as a dressy sport coat. For dress, casual occasions.

Pleated trousers with quality trimmings. Waldes zipper. No vest. Choose from medium blue or light brown.

2. Ties:

Wide ties were all the rage in 1954. Men's ties featured bold patterns, stripes, and vibrant colors. The tie bar or tie clip became a popular accessory.

3. Hats:

Just as with women's fashion, hats were a common sight for men. The fedora, often worn with a suit, was a classic choice.

4. Casual Wear:

For more casual settings, men embraced sports jackets and slacks. These outfits allowed for a relaxed yet put-together appearance.

Youth Fashion:

1. Teenagers:

Teenagers began to establish their own fashion identity. For girls, full skirts and bobby socks were popular, while boys often sported jeans and leather jackets, inspired by the rebelliousness of figures like James Dean.

2. Rock 'n' Roll Style:

The emerging rock 'n' roll culture influenced fashion, with young people adopting leather jackets, white T-shirts, and blue jeans as iconic attire.

3. Sweaters:

Sweaters were a unisex fashion item, often worn with skirts or slacks. Cardigans and crew-neck sweaters were particularly favored.

4. Saddle Shoes:

Saddle shoes, with their distinctive two-tone design, were a footwear choice for both boys and girls.

Evening Wear:
1. Cocktail Dresses:
For formal occasions, women embraced cocktail dresses. These knee-length or tea-length dresses featured elegant cuts and often had embellishments like sequins or lace.

2. Tuxedos:
Men donned tuxedos for evening events. Black tie attire remained a classic choice, exuding sophistication.

Color Palette:
The color palette of 1954 was a mix of soft pastels and bold, vibrant colors. While pastel shades like powder blue and blush pink remained popular for daywear, evening attire often featured rich jewel tones like emerald green and sapphire blue.

5.2 Entertainment and Hobbies

The leisure pursuits and pastimes of 1954 were a reflection of an era poised on the cusp of cultural transformation. People sought enjoyment, relaxation, and ways to connect with family and friends in the post-World War II world. Here's a glimpse into the entertainment and hobbies that captivated hearts and minds in '54:

1. Television Takes Center Stage:

Television continued its ascent as the dominant form of entertainment. Families gathered around their TV sets to watch popular. Television became a window to the world, bringing news, comedy, drama, and music into living rooms across the nation.

2. Radio Remained Relevant:

While television gained prominence, radio remained a vital source of entertainment. People tuned in to their favorite radio programs, enjoying dramas, as well as music on programs.

3. Movie Magic:

Going to the movies was a beloved pastime. The silver screen showcased iconic films like "White Christmas," "Rear Window," and "On the Waterfront." The experience of watching a movie in a theater, complete with popcorn and the latest Hollywood releases, was a cherished tradition.

4. Music and Dance:

Music was a source of joy and a means of expression. The jukebox was a common sight in diners and soda shops, offering the latest hits. People danced to the tunes of Elvis Presley, Frank Sinatra, and Nat King Cole. Rock 'n' roll emerged as a cultural force, igniting a new era of music and youth culture.

5. Reading for Pleasure:

Reading remained a popular leisure activity. Bestsellers like "Lord of the Flies" by William Golding and "The Lord of the Rings" by J.R.R Toikien captured imaginations. Comic books, particularly superhero comics, were a favorite among young readers.

6. Hobbies and Collectibles:

Hobbies took various forms, from stamp and coin collecting to model building and gardening. Many enjoyed the art of crafting and knitting, creating handmade items. Collecting baseball cards and trading them with friends was a common pastime among youngsters.

7. Sports Spectacles:

Sports events offered thrills and camaraderie. Baseball games, boxing matches, and horse races drew enthusiastic crowds. The 1954 World Cup in Switzerland and the Cleveland Indians' participation in the World Series were major sporting highlights.

8. Travel and Adventure:

The allure of travel and exploration was evident as families hit the road for road trips and vacations. Route 66 beckoned as the "Main Street of America," leading travelers to iconic destinations.

Activity:
Fashion Design Coloring Page – Create Your '54-Inspired Outfit

Chapter 6:
Technological Advancements and Popular Cars

6.1 Innovations That Shaped the Future

Solar Cell USA also called photo voltaic cells

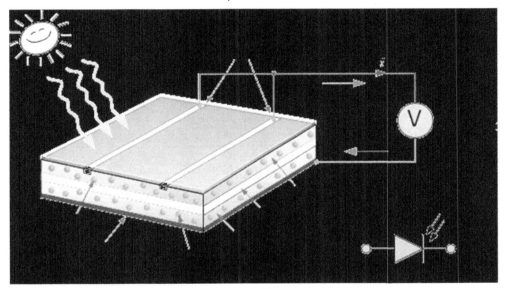

Robot USA by George C Devol Jr

RCA CT-100 Color TV:

RCA began production of its first color TV sets for consumers, the CT-100. The CT-100 had a 15-inch screen and sold for about $1000.

Children receive first mass polio vaccinations, developed by Dr.Jonas Salk

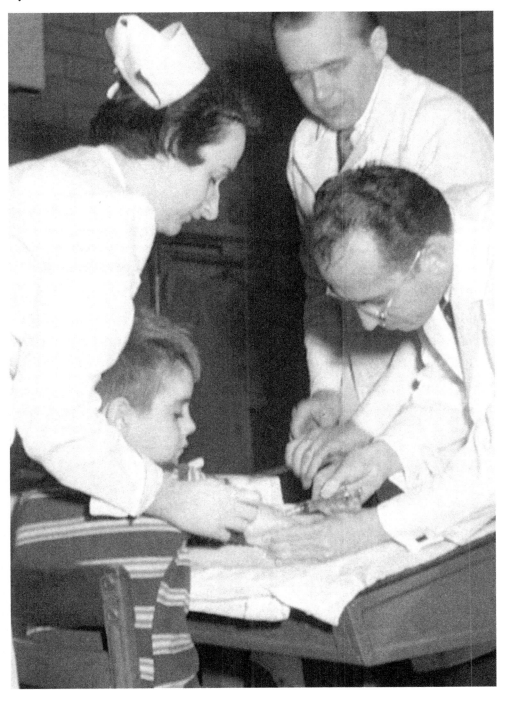

6.2 The Automobiles of '54

In 1954, the American automobile industry was in full swing, producing a wide range of stylish and innovative cars that cap tured the imagination of the public. Here are some of the top automobiles of '54 that left a lasting impression:

Chevrolet Bel Air:

The Chevrolet Bel Air was a true classic of the era, known for its sleek lines and iconic chrome accents. It was available in various body styles, including a convertible and a hardtop coupe, making it a popular choice among American families.

Ford Crestline:

Ford's Crestline series featured distinctive styling with a prominent grille and attractive two-tone color options. It was considered a premium offering in Ford's lineup and boasted V8 engine options for added power.

Buick Skylark:

The Buick Skylark was a symbol of luxury and elegance in 1954. It featured a convertible body style, wire wheels, and upscale interior appointments. The Skylark was Buick's response to the demand for stylish, high-end cars.

Cadillac Eldorado:

The Cadillac Eldorado was the epitome of luxury in '54. Known for its bold styling and powerful V8 engine, the Eldorado was a status symbol. It also introduced features like power windows and seats, setting new standards for automotive comfort.

Chrysler New Yorker:

Chrysler's New Yorker was a full-sized sedan that combined comfort and performance. It featured a distinctive grille and a powerful Hemi V8 engine. The New Yorker was a favorite among those seeking a balance of luxury and performance.

Dodge Royal:

The Dodge Royal was a mid-range offering from Dodge but still packed a punch. It featured a clean, conservative design and was available in various body styles, including sedans and coupes.

Plymouth Belvedere:

The Plymouth Belvedere was a family-friendly car with a straightforward design. It was known for its reliability and affordability, making it a popular choice for budget-conscious buyers.

Oldsmobile Rocket 88:

The Oldsmobile Rocket 88 was famous for its powerful Rocket V8 engine, which contributed to its nickname. It was a sporty and stylish option, known for its performance on the road.

Pontiac Chieftain:

The Pontiac Chieftain featured Pontiac's trademark silver streak styling and offered a balance of style and affordability. It was available in multiple body styles, including sedans and station wagons.

Studebaker Commander:

Studebaker's Commander series was known for its clean and modern design. It featured a bullet-nose front end and offered a comfortable and smooth ride.

Activity: Cars 1954 - Wordsearch

Introduction: Find the names of popular car models from 1954 in the puzzle below

```
E K D A Y I W P Z N W M B N J W R W K A G T J L
J F R A U T A N T T F U Y V G R J A X L T T Z D
L L D V I U E B J D V O D U G S J X W X F G K C
J F Q F P B Y B T R A V E L X Q K G N I D H F H
R C T J L Q A V N V O V Z H P T T W D P U H W G
M K E R V T H W O H Y J V A U T O M O B I L E T
Z W A C D Y O R L R D K A E G T I Z N D H W S W
S K O T M V J L R M T K C B Z R E K B Y H N O M
K H N B L I N X H D P X B L Z Z L K U O I E M O
T F B J W C Y H B S Z N T S U B F Q Y A B W F C
D I B W Y M P T Q I N V E N T I O N T S A F T Z
E W V J Y E W I R P E A B G C P E Z R H T N T W
Q B D T U C A U J E Q E G C Y E P L M M X I H E
C R T B J T R Y M W Q Y P M O M G C Y X Y A E E
S X E G W Y V G E X B X O P A M I J G O C S M X
S F J R K F M P N A N T P K B M N N V M U C S V
N E B D V B Q G G R L X X E W A U Z Z N U J T E
A E Q Y L T R X I Z K L T O C H L U M N P L S H
U N U D L O D F N E X R A S Y U K I E M C D B I
R G Y H S I Q P E A R H K E H O W N G B X E S C
Z I S L E C Z N E J O I F V N Y Z A Y P K Y W L
L N Q H A G H W R V L O V X T T T Y R T U R E E
A E D Y N W K L S T R L X G W H E E L S Z D A L
T A E U B A P E B J N Y C U J Q V E Z R C L W C
```

invention	fast	engineer
automobile	new	old
wheels	travel	karl benz
engine	vehicle	car

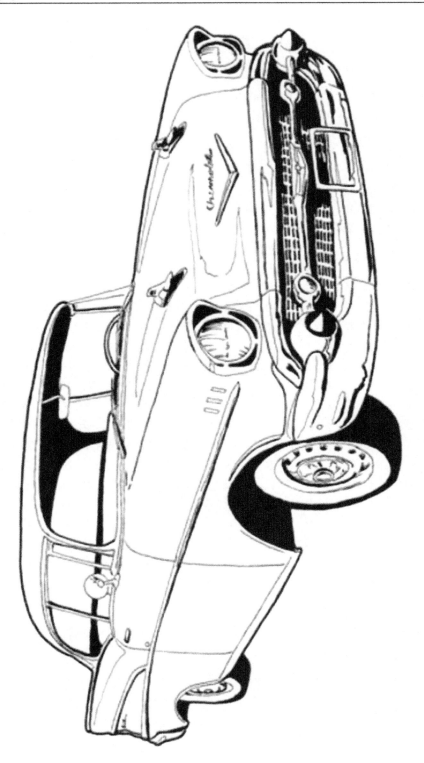

Chapter 7:
Stats and the Cost of Things

7.1 Cost of Living in 1954
Average Cost of new house $10,250.00

.Average Cost of Rent $85.00 per month
.Average wages per year $4,100.00
.Average Cost of a new car $1,700.00
.Movie Ticket 70 cents

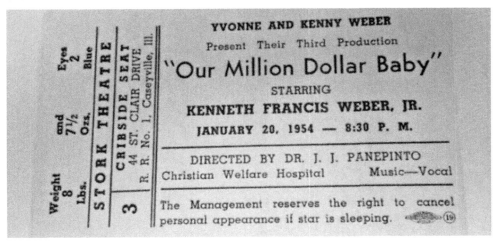

.Life Magazine - 20 cents

.Cost of a gallon of Gas 21 cents
.Postage Stamp 3 cents
.A loaf of bread 17 cents

.Cost of a gallon of milk $0.92

.Bananas 27 cents for 2 pounds

.Eggs per dozen $0.27

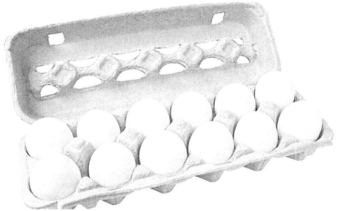

.Swiss cheese $0.69 for 2 pounds

7.2 Inflation and Its Effects

In 1954, the economic landscape of the United States and the United Kingdom was marked by modest inflation rates, offering a sense of stability after the turbulent economic events of the previous decades. Let's delve into the world of inflation and its effects on both sides of the Atlantic, as well as a significant milestone in the world of finance:

1. Yearly Inflation Rate in the USA: 0.32%

The United States experienced a remarkably low inflation rate in 1954, with prices rising by a mere 0.32% annually. This modest inflation contributed to a sense of economic steadiness, assuring consumers that the purchasing power of their dollars remained relatively constant. It was a stark contrast to the double-digit inflation that would trouble economies in the coming decades.

2. Yearly Inflation Rate in the UK: 1.9%

Across the Atlantic, the United Kingdom saw a slightly higher but still manageable inflation rate of 1.9% in 1954. This rate signaled that prices in the UK were rising at a slightly faster pace than in the United States. However, it remained a far cry from the hyperinflation witnessed in some European countries during earlier periods.

3. The Dow Jones Recovers to Pre-Wall Street Crash Highs: 381.17

A significant financial milestone in 1954 was the Dow Jones Industrial Average (DJIA) recovering to pre-Wall Street Crash highs. The DJIA, a key indicator of the stock market's performance, had endured the dramatic crash of 1929 and the subsequent Great Depression. By reaching a level of 381.17, it not only rebounded but also surpassed its pre-crash heights, symbolizing the resilience and recovery of the American economy.

Activity: 1954 Guess the price

Can you guess what each item cost back in 1954?

Cinema ticket
$_____

Gallon of milk
$_____

Dozen eggs
$_____

Postage stamp
$_____

Loaf of bread
$_____

Average house
$_____

Average car
$_____

Gallon of fuel
$_____

Chapter 8:
Iconic Advertisements of 1954

8.1 Remembering Vintage Ads
Mobilgas Ad

Only Gas of its Kind_Boosts Engine Power up to 25%*

Mobilgas SPECIAL

DOUBLE POWERED

1 Mobil Power Compound

2 Top Octane

Mobilgas

There's a Tune-Up in Every Tankful

Vintage 1954 Jell-o Salad Print Ad

Curtiss Candy Company Miracle Aid Wall Art Print Ad

Large Car Ad 1954 Plymouth

Peter Stuyvesant Cigarettes

8.2 Slogans That Stood the Test of Time
Coca-Cola: "It couldn't be better"

In 1954, Coca-Cola introduced the slogan "It couldn't be better." This slogan was part of Coca-Cola's ongoing efforts to emphasize the refreshing and satisfying qualities of their drink. It conveyed the idea that enjoying a Coke was an un-paralleled experience of delight. While this particular slogan may not be as widely remembered today, Coca-Cola's marketing has consistently focused on the themes of happiness, to-getherness, and refreshment, making their brand enduringly popular.

1954 7Up Advertisement: "Fresh up with Seven up!"

Seven-Up's iconic slogan from 1954, "Fresh up with Seven-Up!" has left a lasting mark in the world of advertising. This slogan was catchy and memorable, emphasizing the refreshing and invigorating qualities of the lemon-lime soda. Even today, variations of this slogan are occasionally used in marketing and advertising campaigns for 7Up. It's a testament to the enduring appeal of a simple, yet effective, advertising message.

Activity: Design your own slogan

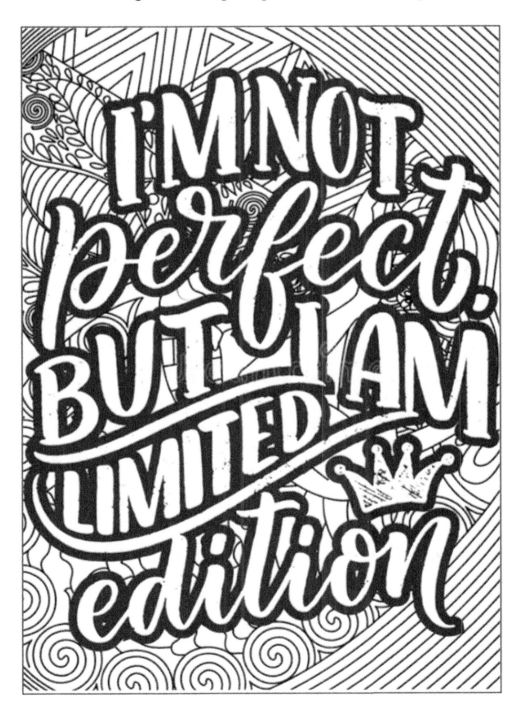

We have heartfelt thank-you gifts for you

As a token of our appreciation for joining us on this historical journey through 1954, we've included a set of cards and stamps inspired by the year of 1954. These cards are your canvas to capture the essence of the past. We encourage you to use them as inspiration for creating your own unique cards, sharing your perspective on the historical moments we've explored in this book. Whether it's a holiday greeting or a simple hello to a loved one, these cards are your way to connect with the history we've uncovered together.

Happy creating!

Activity Answers:
Chapter 1:
1. BROWN
2. KHRUSHCHEV
3. HARBOR
4. SECURITY
5. CENSURE
6. FORCES
7. HO CHI MINH
8. NASSER
9. NEHRU
10. ALLEGIANCE
Chapter 2:
1. c) White Christmas
2. a) Alfred Hitchcock
3. a) On the Waterfront
4. c) Marilyn Monroe
5. a) Humphrey Bogart
6. c) Walt Disney's Wonderful World of Color
7. c) The Andersons
8. a) Mailroom clerk
9. a) Gail Davis
10. d) From Here to Eternity
11. c) George Alfred Mitchell
Chapter 3:
1. "cutest"
2. "hill"
3. "paradise"
4. "warth"; "petals"
5. "stars"; "fool"

Chapter 4:

1. b) West Germany
2. d) New York Giants
3. b) Syracuse Nationals
4. c) Veikko Karvonen
5. a) Juan Manuel Fangio
6. b) Cleveland Browns
7. c) Rocky Marciano
8. b) Detroit Red Wings

Embracing 1954: A Grateful Farewell

Thank you for joining us on this journey through a year that holds a special place in our hearts. Whether you experienced 1954 firsthand or through the pages of this book, we hope it brought you moments of joy, nostalgia, and connection to a time that will forever shine brightly in our memories.

Share Your Thoughts and Help Us Preserve History

Your support and enthusiasm for this journey mean the world to us. We invite you to share your thoughts, leave a review, and keep the spirit of '54 alive. As we conclude our adventure, we look forward to more journeys through the annals of history together. Until then, farewell and thank you for the memories.

We would like to invite you to explore more of our fantastic world by scanning the QR code below. There you can easily get free ebooks from us and receive so many surprises.

TO DO LIST

- ○ ------------------------------
- ○ ------------------------------
- ○ ------------------------------
- ○ ------------------------------
- ○ ------------------------------
- ○ ------------------------------
- ○ ------------------------------
- ○ ------------------------------
- ○ ------------------------------
- ○ ------------------------------
- ○ ------------------------------
- ○ ------------------------------
- ○ ------------------------------
- ○ ------------------------------

well done!

TO DO List

- [ ]
- [ ]
- [ ]
- [ ]
- [ ]
- [ ]
- [ ]
- [ ]
- [ ]
- [ ]
- [ ]
- [ ]
- [ ]

To Do List

TO DO LIST

- ○ ---
- ○ ---
- ○ ---
- ○ ---
- ○ ---
- ○ ---
- ○ ---
- ○ ---
- ○ ---
- ○ ---
- ○ ---
- ○ ---
- ○ ---
- ○ ---

well
done!

TO DO LIST

Name: _____   Day: _____   Month: _____

No	To Do List	Yes	No

NOTE

NOTE

NOTE

NOTE

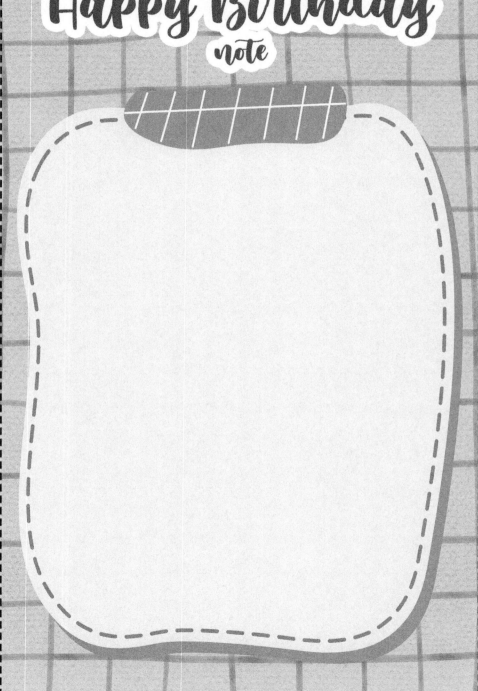

Happy Birthday

note

Happy Birthday
note

HAPPY BIRTHDAY NOTE

POSTCARD

Correspondence

Address

POSTCARD

To:

From:

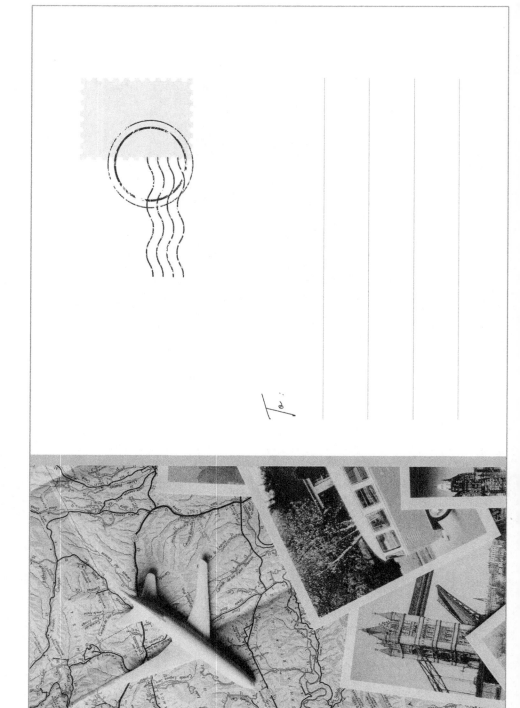

Remember This!

WISH YOU WERE HERE,
123 ANYWHERE ST., ANY CITY

Printed in Great Britain
by Amazon

42831123R00069